peeled

peeled
SUBHADASSI

Arc
PUBLICATIONS
2004

Published by Arc Publications
Nanholme Mill, Shaw Wood Road
Todmorden OL14 6DA, UK

www.arcpublications.co.uk

Design by Tony Ward
Print by Antony Rowe Ltd.,
Eastbourne, East Sussex

ISBN 1 900072 87 4

Acknowledgements:

'Magpie' was written for an Encore commission in 2002 funded by Northern Arts, WWT Washington, Sunderland Council and New Writing
North; 'Carmen' was written during an Arts Council of England Year of
the Artist residency at the Wildfowl and Wetlands Trust, Washington,
2000 funded by Northern Arts, Sunderland Council, WWT and New
Writing North; 'Multi Story', 'Country and Western' and 'Oracle' were
written as 'poems on the Metro' for a Year of the Artist residency on the
Tyne and Wear Metro, 2000 funded by Northern Arts and Nexus; 'Ambit'
was written on a Poetry Society *Poetry Places* residency in the Port of
Sunderland, 2000; 'A Sense of Grace' was written for *Beyond Belief*, Dur-
ham Literature Festival 2000. 'Angel of the City' appears in the poetry
film *ODE*, commissioned by Graingertown, Newcastle, 1998; 'Ontology'
was inspired by Geshe Rabten's commentary on the Heart Sutra. The
epigraph to 'Subtext' appears in *The Rag and Bone Shop of the Heart*, ed.
Robert Bly *et al*. An untitled photograph by Stephen Batchelor that ap-
peared in *Dharma Life* magazine inspired 'The Middle of Nowhere';
'Dutch Landscape with Skaters' was published in *Urthona* magazine;
'Museo Garcia Lorca', 'Subtext' and 'Simple Harmonic Motion' were
published in *Envoi* magazine; 'Release the Bats' and 'Treason' were published in *moodswing* magazine; 'Turn Off your Phone' was published in
Staple magazine.

I would like to thank Linda France, Jo Shapcott, Claire Malcolm (Director
of New Writing North), and Andy Croft for their help and support.

The Publishers acknowledge financial
assistance from ACE Yorkshire

Editor for UK / Ireland: Jo Shapcott

*for my parents
Tommy and Jean Dixon,
with love*

This all night, this all night,
every night an' all;
fire and fleet and candle light,
and Christ take up thy soul.

When thou from hence away art past,
every night an' all;
to Whinnymoor thi comes at last,
and Christ take up thy soul.

If ever thi's given socks er shoes,
every night an' all;
sit thi down an' put 'em on
an' Christ take up thy soul.

If socks er shoes thi never give none,
every night an' all;
winds'll prick thee through t'bone
an' Christ take up thy soul…

…This all night, this all night,
every night an' all;
fire and fleet and candle light,
and Christ take up thy soul.

from *The Lyke Wake Dirge*

Contents

The Chapatti Trick

In the beginning was Vesta. Small packets
full of dubious matter to hydrate, boil,
mix together: extra chemistry lessons
on Sundays; my Mum's *one night off.*
Then onto the earth tottered Chicken Bhuna.
Friday night was a gallon of Tetley's,
Sher-e-Punjab by the Station. If provoked
– I often was – I performed The Chapatti Trick.
Now I play God on a weekend. Before starting
to cook I seed an Indian visualisation
to locate inspiration: is it Madras or Bengali;
Basmati or Idli? Grind my own spices,
oil my kharai: bring the matter in hand
to two mouths starved in the act of Creation.

Dakini Over New York ————————————

When I found the email was from Martha Vine
– tech' manager for some digital recording site –
I was surprised to find, alongside facts about lasers
and lead-in times, a recipe for yam and cinnamon bagels.

And though my life is often like a subway train
that morning I was free, so after T'ai Chi I threw
together the dough, left it to rise by the east window
(Manhattan in full swing below), plumped my cushions,
lit a stick of incense – Indian, powder of a thousand
flower blossoms – and entered meditation.

She was garlanded with skulls and the sky's acetylene,
in her left hand the Statue of Liberty, in her right a flaying knife.
I was just accustoming myself to her breasts
– the way her nipples made flaming circles as she swayed
above the tower blocks – when she began:

firstly a cut round the thick of my thighs like a garter;
two others to girdle my neck and belly so true they were painless.
She stripped me back to something out of Gray's Anatomy,
a dance of death full of her mix of bliss and emptiness.

Risen, I shaped the bagels, watched each one swim to the surface
of the boiling water then baked them in the oven.
All I can say is I saw things different: alive less to each zero
of soft bread flesh; more to the freedom which seeded it –
that hole in its middle. The light at the end of her tunnel.

the Buddha wanders through Sandhill,
under the arches on Dean Street,
just makes it up Dog Leap, his Minidisc playing
the theme tune from *Get Carter*.

He catches a Zebra to the Head Of Steam:
orders a Guinness which he sips very slowly,
gazing out of the window at a black cab,
asking himself what it is that *makes* them –

the shape, chassis, FARE sign or the driver
reading a library book – what you could take away.
With the back of his hand he wipes off his foam moustache.
Steps outside, leaving no tracks.

Siren

You skim the dual carriageway – it offers you the city –
hit a roundabout too quickly, part the stream

of steel and rubber with a screech: the gods are with you.
Or are they? As you sailed over the circle

your mind seemed to pour through its own eye
and you lost one-point perspective;

ten thousand things streamed through you.
You were the bridge and all its rivets;

the *mee maa* of an ambulance upon it; an eddy
in the river underneath, each molecule of water;

the dark blood on your own windscreen.
And finally you got it: dead.

Drawn to what you love, you marinated in the colours
of the Quayside bars' neon signs:

plumbed cerulean blue; rode their voltages
inside to find the young in one another's arms

where, non-Euclidean, you danced on a pinhead –
the jukebox's laser; fathomed the music;

flew higher: without a fight
took leave of your senses one last time.

In the lumpen world of matter you shall blossom
in the central reservation: white lilies hitched to a barrier

plucking the conscience of each passing driver
as they improvise that adverse camber.

Sky Burial

When the body dies there is no need to keep it.
Wood is scarce; the ground all frost.

He burned charcoal, sticks of juniper for incense;
in the rhythm of a mantra cut meat from her bones:

the vultures' turns tightened at the scrape of his hatchet;
with a flick of his wrist he invited them to breakfast.

And he strives to realise the increases she met in death
within his placid mind, his ruddy flesh

while the birds – much quicker to digest –
drop strings of bloody pearls over the snowfields of Tibet.

Cygnus————————————————

Here may be seen how being blessed
Has its foundations in the act of sight,
And not in love, which comes afterwards.
                    Dante *Paradiso XXVIII* 109-11

If I were half-blind, which I am –
my eye-world dropping-off to shapes
no more than vague suggestions,
the *all-that-is-in-the-detail* lost

so that my fingers must become
precision instruments to skim surfaces,
assist in weighings to confirm hunches –
then in these days that blur to nights

and nights that linger, my skin would come
in search of you: follow your scent,
lock-on to your body heat sensed in my palms
like a prickle or an ache, that would not fade

till it lighted on, say, a braid, or nap:
the down at the back of your neck,
perhaps. Corroborating evidence,
I'd map that rare constellation

mazed in the freckles in your back
– sole vantage offered from your bed –
knowing full-well that this would turn
all the lights back on again.

Annealed ─────────────────

He plugged the window's hole with honeycomb
against the wind and sleet from Uzbekistan;
pumped the leather bellows with his feet and hands,
eager for the iron to find *pomegranate red:*
the colour that was good for the plunge into honey.

The sweet steam took him back to the harvest fair
and the girl – he'd thought of her as Liesl –
who sold him enough for the winter;
told him that bees made love and that made honey.

Honey that made a metal fit to shoe the Meister's horses;
fit for the horses to spark the black volcanic stones of Slovakia
as they cantered through his forests with an ooze
of hounds around them, welded to a scent of fox.

He licked honey from the edge of his knife:
a blade that would never go blunt; her sting he would
$$\text{never pull out.}$$

A Sense of Grace ————————————

It's like you've just been born.
Your spine uncurls like a fern;
the delicate skin under each of your eyes
hasn't even had time to dry.

Time's taken off her roller blades,
woken up to the size of the sky.
Tomorrow waits patiently,
like a performing dog, for a sign.

Light Pollution, Loch Voil ——————

After hours of plumbing cloudless midnight steel,
odd Borealis sparks, I made it up the hill,
turned to the south to find a pair of orange blurs
at the horizon: Edinburgh's loose change;
the leftovers of cold Glasgow. A million sodium lights
which at that distance lit no roads.
Come five the sky's night shades – natural
or otherwise – were shown back to their homes
by the one who'd idly spun high cirrus
to a shoal of rainbow trout; then tickled them
with her slim, long-imagined rosy fingers.

At Crothà Bothy ————————————

First you hear them: their song-lines
ring over rocks to your well-rinsed ears.
Furred-in by peat, dug deep in the hillside,
some sound guttural, cock-sure;
so deep in the earth it's become instrumental:
didgeridoos to the circular breathing of water.
Those nearer the surface are less certain;
pipe nervous falsettos.
                                  Regardless,
each one tips-up its silver in the river
running naked and noisy way down in the bottom.
It echoes round basalt, under bridges:
voices break in the waterfall, hush
into the lochan. From there it's all downhill
to the boom of the ocean.

Fief

I've had it up to here –
this bloody hat.

Jacobite, she said,
the first time I'd got near enough

to smell her.
I will not wear it.

I have doffed myself
off my own map. It is time to put

back on my green felt cap.
Pull it right down over my ears.

Fishing

I tackle-up. My mind's all carp: slick slow-movers
mottled with leather, or mirror. We're armed to the teeth
with par-boiled potatoes and honey, a killer
combination, but this morning nothing's biting.

An aeon later, frozen, walking legs like someone else's
up the steps, I look back to find the pond haloed
by spindles of silver birch; catch one big spare rib of a ripple sounding
its length. I'm spell-bound. Something's stirring.

Dutch Landscape with Skaters ──────────

I am looking from the green tower's window
onto the ice. The skin on my face is taut, it has grown
a fur of frost; my buttocks are warm from the hearth.
Today everything sounds sharp – the sweep of skates on bends,
the shrill of the vicar's girls, creaking masts.

I am full of regret for the pleasures Piotr and I have yet
to share. I will him to canter through the birch wood
past wattle-and-daub; tether his master's horse;
slip round the back of the manse to find my cold cheeks
with his hot hands: give me something to be ashamed of.

Simple Harmonic Motion ———————

For me it is the acme, the Indian Summer
of her brassière: its abdication
from her breasts, their blush and dusk
as the rest of her garments shrink
to rags draped on the wardrobe;
rags with which her body has shared
intimacies, whose textures played
around her, breathed Givenchy and oestrogen.
Silently she lies there: a small serenity
about her, afloat on her very own ocean,
the Queen Size duvet's tidal wave
of *soft*, of *happy*. Night-flowering red lotus.

Mango

Holding it against a skinny thigh he cut through peel,
began his search for the edge of the stone with the steel,

describing its arc in flesh so keen to secede from bone.
He carved a pair of orange worlds second to none

then scored them – buttery, the Deccan's best –
before a nimble flick of the wrist to make concave convex

so he could free the chunks with his tongue and teeth,
encourage the pulp against his throat and mouth.

It grew sweeter with each bite. Ripe-bellied, at ease,
he would doze on red dust amid a halo of flies,

the nimbus of shed skins parched to sickle moons
by the time he blinked himself alive.

Background Radiation ———————

I cast nylon line into the river's rust-brown;
took a tumble. My Dad, one pitch down, dropped his rod,
followed on. Though currents pulled me under
I stayed calm: went along with them all till they spat
me out. I bobbed-up like a buoy.

His blue-collar hands lugged me to the bank;
I was just winded. His army watch – gunmetal grey –
was the only casualty, its bezel flooded.
The next day we found a jeweller who'd polish
its seventeen diamonds. He wouldn't take any money.

Now I wear it, this watch that survived
North African sands; saw Mussolini swinging from a gibbet –
hours I'd never told till I laid it by my bed
that very first time. I switched on the night
and its face stranged my own with astringent light.

Room 33, British Museum ──────────

Just beyond the village jurisdiction
he spent each day working-up the ores;
took only one or two disciples who would learn
to quarry, sweat the rocks with charcoal,
pour pools of flawless mirror.

Warriors came, performed libations,
petitioned him to mend their weapons
in return for rice, stared at his hair;
ran back to their settlements, their wives,
flaunting the knives' bright blades.

Each full-moon dusk he'd bring his furnace
up to heat, sing iron and bronze into their moulds.
In the cooling air he'd hatch fine fetishes
from clay upholding love, not war,
which even at ten paces remind me what I bother for.

Compass ―――――――――――――――――――――

I'll give you an old game that's in two halves; wings to lift
you off the page: a crow with something shiny in its beak.

Follow its slip-stream to a nest-egg: your birth-right.

No longer all tongue-tied, you'll be whistled and feathered
for the short-haul north to your skin: a new home.

peeled ——————————————————————

an time when a said a could take all me clothes off
cos I felt so open even though it were october
an you lot took piss for a decade –
that night when a put too many mushrooms in pan
second a heard me dad reversin out o drive
an you lot came out o woodwork

an wi loads o sugar'n'milk'n'nescaf
wi downed it in a oner an got right outa there,
away from semis; through intake an golcar flats
over scar lane an onto edge
where weavers cottages windows were searin red
an a took a piss in british legion car park
an knew it were comin on cos pissin
were like growin a stalk o wheat

an across valley slawit were meltin
into marsden an pike were screechin
wi laughter an lal were goin bendy
an scad were lost as per usual an wilf cun't talk
as per usual an all shamanic gridsndots like in cave paintins
nmiros neverythinbloodyelse it seems just now
were soarin through us fields o vision

an we stopped at old sandstone steps by canal
to weigh stone that were left
an stone thatd been worn bi millions o millworkers feet
leavin a curve o empty space an wi concluded
thi were exactly equal down to a milligram

an it came on really strong as we fumbled
down t appleyards – we were talkin g force six –
an the wer police sirens hung in trees
an when we got there us lager guzzled itself in corner
so we sat on bench except scad who sat on is arse
starin down canal an saying *but where are we really*

an even though us pupils still teemed us faces
you cruelly took piss an all innocence left yer
when a said a could take all me clothes off.
Its outlived us crimped hair us docks us schoolin;
us smiths albums us girlfriends us drug habits –
in most cases us friendships.
                                                Well, I meant it.

Road ————————————————————————————

Skelter down from the seventh floor of the multi-storey;
hang a right to find the central motorway. Follow
the ribbon of red brake lights round the elementary
                                        mathematics
of the carriageways; take the slip road for the A69
– it slits England's throat from ear to ear –
but don't go the full distance: let Hadrian's Wall reassure you
with antiquity as you spin down the Military Road.

After an indefinable time wade through two gates;
find the neon apples of lambs' eyes ripening
on your full beam; indignant rabbits staring from the fell.
As you activate the central-locking look up at the gable
of the cottage: decipher where she is; what she's perfecting
with nimble fingers in her province of yellow light.
Know any road would have brought you home tonight.

Ontology

Things such as jugs, clothes, tents,
armies, forests, rosaries, trees,
dwellings, trolleys and Guest Houses
you should understand to exist
in the way they are commonly talked of.
The Great One did not argue over these matters:
they serve their purpose just as,
even though a reflection is not real,
it can still tell you your face is dirty.
However, by applying the parable of the broom
to people, with their attachment and desires
– fire and the fuel that it burns –
you will find that they do not exist
in any of the seven ways. In the rays
of wisdom emerging from such analyses
you will glimpse the truth of the three worlds
as clearly as you can see a green olive
resting in the palm of your hand.

Birds

My grandmother carried her burden
for thirty years, then one afternoon
as she carried her shopping home
it lifted off her *like a bird – just like that,*
she said the one time she mentioned it.
The last time we met she wasn't ackled
right all afternoon. She pointed
to some rooks above the telly that I had
to say weren't there; her mind dispersing,
lifting away from her. When the vicar said
Ashes, I cried into my palms, very quietly.

This is no iron angel. On the day it floated out
into the Wear no-one shouted *Eureka*. It started raining.

Sixty years ago, crowds lined Wearmouth Bridge
to watch Austin's Pontoon snake-charm Colliers –

leave them high and dry for riveters who'd learned lip-reading
in the shriek of steel to restore Archimedes' principle

to the ships with weld and elbow grease.
Now Wreath Quay Road's recycled. Ambit's single eye

would be lucky to find one little fishing boat.
Its stainless lips are pursed to a *Makkem* O –

the O in *loss, gone. Scapegoat.* The present's full
of sculpture heaped with the sins of global economics

at the mercy of the tides, the wrath of proud Sunderland.
Now the kids don't even miss the ships, don't know what sisal is.

For them the river's to throw stones in, those silver lips
something to aim at from the crescent moon of Burdon's bridge.

'Ambit', a major public artwork by Alison Wilding, was built in Sunderland and sited in the River Wear in September 1999. The site for-
merly housed Austin's shipyard where, until 1966, the vast structure
of Austin's Pontoon was regularly submerged and re-floated in order
to raise huge ships from the water for repair. Ambit is 20 metres in
length and describes the outline of a ship.

Art on the Riverside (Online)

This is the town that killed its poet.
They'd never seen his colour before.
Oh how I want you, green.

They've never seen it since.
Shade of a sigh;
the sigh of wind through olives in the Albaicín.

He wanted to die in *Holland sheets,*
an iron bed. He was shot
in the back of the head; tossed

in an unmarked grave at four a.m.
A horse without a mount
thunders its heart out on the plain.

It Didn't Have To End Like This ——————

i.m. Andrew Waterhouse, 1958-2001

It didn't have to end like this.
The fact is that it did. Your skin,
the pores on your nose, that way you looked
sidelong just to check that things
were as they'd been moments before.
Feral, tentative, all ears.

Hammer, anvil, stirrup.
I suffer your bones in a carrier bag as I walk
across the fell, seeking the right spot
to sow them. White seeds, they rattle me.
I know they will not grow. It's been two years.
It didn't have to end like this.

Kindness

The road is a tongue of cinders daubed in tarmac.
It uncurls up the hill to the North Cliff.
The earth, abrupt beside it, orange after rain,
snakes a gradient even the oldest bones can negotiate.

Kindness is a small dog with burnished bristles
wagging its tail, following an old woman
through the palm trees' shade.

At the clifftop, where the ocean is an idea of blue,
the road flattens, spreads itself.
She faces the sun, her eyes focusing
down to the beach, the glint of fishermen.

Mr and Mrs Calypso ────────────────

By five it was cool enough to think
and in wild thyme honey coloured light
I saw each pebble in the bay
was made of the self-same marble
as the effigies we'd tracked down earlier.

Lucent, primitive, hers had arms cradling
an ocean belly, exquisite in the hushed museum.
Mine was still in the rock it was born from –
Kouros, fifteen metres high, left for us to chance
upon by its flaws, inadequate for export.

In the modest shade of the purple fig
we'd yielded to each other's pluck and peel;
then buttock to buttock read the biggest
hardback books the beach had ever seen.
Mr and Mrs Calypso in the factor twenty sun.

No distant wife unpicking herself each night,
no same thing twice. After a month we caught
the night boat, waved goodbye to gulls flapping
themselves backwards off the cliffs.
Left the oldest of myths.

Multi Story ——————————————

It's no heaven, but when concrete streams
were calmed to slabs, sculpting a cube visible
for miles, our minds grew full under its promise.

Even Caine, as *Carter*, was drawn North on a train
to drink from a thin glass, corkscrew up nine flights
in a sporty white number to put things straight.

Now rust bleeds from the elephant's skin.
Its lifts are tired. A stone's throw from the seventh floor
a slick new bridge articulates the Tyne.

Country and Western ——————

He signs his name in red by the Metro sign –
four letters, *SLIM* – then makes his way downstairs
into the ten gallon weather with a pair
of Levi's and his new silver mobile.
It plays a tune he calls *The Cavalry*:
he draws it from his holster like a gun.
The message says *stay on God's Train, my son*.
He's cactus-lonely, tears freeze in his eyes:
those words tell Slim his Daddy's upped and gone
just like he said he would some winter day,
leaving him to live with his ol' Mom.
The minutes spin like tumbleweed, away
down railway tracks stark as his lonesome thoughts.
It's the last straw. His phone sparks like a spur
on the platform as he stands clear of the doors.

Oracle

At a time when iron birds circle
trails wide as the Tyne
where many-coloured chariots of steel
are drawn by invisible horses,
invincible but for want of water;

and the birds disgorge their tribes
in black and white on foreign shores
where they will fight among themselves,
suspended in the sky with ocean views,
grow easy on the drink;

at a time when iron houses slide
on shrieking tracks from town to town;
women and men invoke omens
with their shaman's bone held to the ear,
the magic spell *amonthetrain* intoned;

matters of love and loss
shall still tease tender lives apart:
the riddles that goad ours
will vex their town, their homes,
their solitary hearts.

The slick black swan stands on one leg by the pond,
frocked in high-necked taffeta. She is solid flamenco.
Each wing flick castanets black noise. Do not follow
the light from the two dark stars of her eyes.

Angel of the City ——————————

Find your own pace.
Settle into it, loosening while walking.

Feel your feet against the floor,
resist the earth. Rise up,

let the head lead forwards
and your body keep its balance,

knowing the bones are moving
easily under the flesh.

Keep your eyes relaxed,
like two still pools of water.

Be in and of yourself,
contained inside your skin.

When you have found your rhythm,
broaden your attention.

Take in all the people,
such different sorts around you.

And though you're close to them
as breath, no-one will recognise

your moments of absorption
as you pay your respects to the living,

glimpse into the heart of the city's
frail, human ecologies:

forge love, awareness, insight
in a brand new way of walking.

Museo Garcia Lorca, Fuente Vaqueros —

When the bells strike ten, the invisible curator
will appear. In the meantime watch
the balcony's cast-iron crescents locking horns

under the moon's pale semicircle
new-minted into sky's powder blue
from the treasury of the Sierra Nevada.

Through the olivewood door find *membrillos* and *granadas*
in a Moorish bowl on the kitchen table.
Make yourself at home. Go on,

pull up one of the Original Chairs.
Through scent alone find the ripest pomegranate;
cut it open with a blade forged in Albacete:

with its hook of steel cockle-out
the dense galaxy, licking wine from the knife edge
when you've worked its cavities.

Each last fruit eaten, stand up.
Clamber onto the table. Drunk on the liquor
of rubies, full of explicable sadness

scream *Murderers! Murderers!*
for all you're worth till the last chime of noon,
the next bus to Granada, where you'll do something else.

The strip-light flickers on mock-wood panelling.
There is a fish tank. Fish – some Angels –
coast its length. A man leans against the counter
having his way with the last of a tab.
With his heel he turns it into the lino:
one more dark star in the floor's constellation.
Are you having it now or will you take it away?
I am having it now. I will also take it away.

Magpie ⸻

He blunts every shade
of the rainbow to *black* or *white,* knows
exactly what he likes: a nest feathered
with trinkets; the comfort of fool's gold.
In fact he knows it all bar what he won't be told:
that he's stuck, welded inside a shell,
bespoke. Sooner or later he'll choke.
At his age you'd think he'd know better.
He doesn't. It's no joke.

The Middle of Nowhere ——————

It's some time at the end of last century
in a room that is utterly undomestic,

most likely at an airport or conference centre,
the floor a moonscape peopled by wire-frame chairs

whose constellations are all that remains
of their last occupants who have since flown

elsewhere, leaving these frayed brocades of meaning.
Five in the foreground nucleate

around a waste bin, right at the edge of the picture
from which, stage left, you enter;

sit down just in time to catch each metal atom
breaking open, watch the spectacle

of insipid lino giving way to an ocean
from which a mer-girl surfaces. She's half babe,

half dragon-woman: as out of place
in this sanitised arena as she is in your mind's eye,

you sworn non-believer. With a flourish she offers you
a life's work: your head, on a plate.

Her almond eyes incite you to own that first face.
And this time you won't get away.

The Library that Fell into the Sea ————

High noon. A map scratched in the sand – the sort of thing
you only find with no Safeway for a thousand miles.
We follow it, go nowhere in the sundial shadows of the masts,
a cock crowing in perfect Greek;

chart the weather's breath with each pore
in our cinnamon skin – slight changes in the wind,
the day's braille heat, its pulse
of *now* and *now* and *now* and *now*. Wild sesame.

Release the Bats ──────────────

Don't tell me that it doesn't hurt
            'Release the Bats' by The Birthday Party (1981)

I'm awake in my bedroom, though you'd never guess:
it's way past my bed-time and pitch-black
but for two tiny sources of light – windows the size
of matchboxes, a needle drumming the air
to a radio signal that flies here from elsewhere
than this hillside, this village, this estate.

They keep hitting their stops, the VU meters,
the tiny electromagnets that drive them overloaded
with *Babylon's Burning; Longships; Love Will Tear Us Apart
(Again); Inflammable Material; How Soon Is Now?*
Each song real to me as the headphones stuck
with sweat to the side of my head.

Midnight, the pips: I pull the plug, the lights fade.
Secrets, hidden like those dirty books under the bed.

Turn off your phone ————————————————

Turn off your phone.
                       Place it, face down,
on cold sandstone: that oxblood-red back-step
she buffed for sixty years.
                              Look out
past the well-kept lawn, its marrow stripes
while radio waves walk through walls,
bark, bone and steel:
                           congregate to a signal.

Rest your eyes beyond the fence
on the trunks of birch that ebb into the wood.
Feel those white trees breathe.
                         The entropy
of branch and leaf may offer some relief.

Whether they do or don't,
after a time you must pick up your phone,
face its empty screen:
                       turn it on again.

He sailed through fecund jungle – a sea of leaves and creepers,
archipelagos of villages, all bamboo cane and palm leaves.

smells tacked through the carriage – palm oil: cloying, heady;
unfamiliar base notes, coconut and chilli.

Trees disgorged a coastline – fishing boats, blue ocean;
inside, a hawker worked the aisle chanting a *small eats* mantra

until a blind old drummer, her right eyesocket weeping,
pinned his ears against the headrest, drowned all the other clatter.

Her fingers blurred to mirrors. Shaking like the devil she articulated
sticky air till he knew where the hell he was going.

Sigirya Maiden ———————————

He took the rock-cut footings,
navigated spiral stairs keyed into schist
to see her eyes in the flesh,
the promise of her breasts.

She was a survivor.
Though cracks framed her
she remained unweathered:
those knowing almond eyes;
her ears' and wrists' inscrutable gold hoops.

Underneath were love poems:
ancient graffiti on the Mirror Wall.
He didn't understand those tiny bones,
the script: though even if he did

he'd never fathom it.
She is impossible to touch.

*I have seen the victor Dioxippos subdue all contenders at Olympia
and be thrown on his back by the glance of a girl.*

Diogenes

There she was, vying in her innocence behind a skinny latte.
He struggled to suss her, work her out from first principles
whilst complying with her dull pretence that there were no rules,
that all their machinery of longing was spontaneous
along with its promise of *left blank for your own message.*

She bulged with charm. He was under orders. A train worked-up
its shudder on the platform. Soon it would be released
from this city. He longed to slough their charade as easily.
Made as he was of parts softer than steel, his sentence was certain.
For life. In his heart the compromise intrinsic to desire.

Blue Lies

I knew better than to call the sea *irreducible*
or claim it was *endlessly delighting in its own simplicity*.
I was happy not to catch it at all
knowing it was in league with the moon,

that sunbleached goat's horn riding the clouds
as the heat gave the last of itself to the waves
that told the same old story, putting on their silver nets
behind the tamarisks. It was enough to swim in it.

Now I'm the one that's blue,
acting like the tide's gone out forever,
shrunk inside the postcard by my kettle.
Water deeper than a thousand sinks. That nakedness.

Mythos: the Movie ──────────────

In the generous shade of the juniper tree
they can't decide who's playing who, or when:
are they in Star Trek or Don Quixote? Hypnotised by heat
she chooses Dapple, Sancho's donkey – faithful to the end.

He goes for Hadji Murad, liking the sound of him.
Flat on their backs, whirlpool bark spins them asleep
and they're tethered for what seems like the first time ever
after the trial of crossing a dried-up river

in the hum of an alien sun. Rested, they escape ,
to a village, the safety of lemon tea, *kataifi*, the half-way mark.
Back at base they catalogue mutations –
her forty extra freckles, his sun-bleached eyebrows,

call them rites of passage. Cut to the washing
of the pilgrims' feet; the making ready for the final mission.

Treason

Down on the cutting at the edge of the park
we laid new two pence pieces on the tracks,
hid behind rosebay willowherb till the 125 flew past,
found shiny, melted metal scattered in the grass –
their second minting, in the North;

the train by then in the longest tunnel on earth.
Twenty years later it came out, in reverse,
with me in second class. By the same sandstone bridge
I glimpsed two kids on the parallel lines;
felt the weight of loose change in my pocket.

Tell

They say the folk you're with
in the moments you die
somehow typify your life.
Think of Plato with his mates;
Mohammed with thirty wives;
Tommy Cooper on stage;
Diana dogged by *papperazzi*.
If you made a line from now
all the way to your demise
what would it look like?

Imagine: choose a year,
date, place, day of the week;
who would you end up with?
Your spouse? Or lover? Father
or mother? Son or daughter?
Sister or brother? Companions
in some *good life* or other?
Or would it be a solo ride?
Go on: decide.

Sunday

This is a day when even the postman
won't break the skin of silence that we've spread
across the surface of our brand new pond.
Quiet ripples-out into the garden,
slips though the gate all the way down the fell to the pylons.

Pond skaters can't ignore its short-range
attractive forces. Held against gravity, they spin
across its membrane on microclimatic winds.
One of us two would need to be Jesus, or some other
sweet-tongued prophet, to pull a trick off like that one.

Human, we follow two green newts as they dangle
just below the liquid plane, framed by spikes
of blown yellow iris, rowan branch shadows.
In whispers we explain the pool to each other
having till recently believed all waters were born, not made.

We get as far as an account of its shape –
somewhere between *comma* and *Southeast Asian island* –
when rain starts drawing circles: it's time to leave
the wildlife, go in, put the kettle on.
The pond's all peaks and troughs as little waves

interfere destructively, constructively;
the rowan berries' reflections lost for the moment:
that glimpse of ourselves suspended in hard-won water.

The Various Kinds of Unedifying Poems ——

Epistles to kings, robbers, ministers;
dramas about armies, dangers, wars, food, drink, clothes;
lyrics with beds, garlands or perfumes, relatives or carriages in them;
epics regarding villages, towns cities or countries;
sonnets to women, men or heroes;
street and well songs, laments on the deserted;
desultory lyrics, heroic couplets concerning land or sea;
blank verse on being or non-being:
these are the thirty kinds of unedifying poems.

The Beloved —————————————

The erotics of composition are essential to the process.
        Seamus Heaney, *Beowulf*, translator's introduction

When she's had her way, closed her circle
good and proper around him thrice,
fed him her honey, she's off, sharpish.
He's a goner, the house of his body derelict
from a whole month in the sway of her frenzy:
strip-teasing him, shaking those fennel heads;
floating him in her ocean.
                        Boy, he's beached.
Sparks a fire in the wood-stove; stares
out of the window for something to wish on,
knowing full well her own constellation's
down-under, and no space junk will coax her.
He'll just have to mulch, compost
over the winter; prepare for the spring rites:
bone-up on the art of surrender.

Biographical Note —————————————

SUBHADASSI was born in Huddersfield in 1967. After completing a degree in Chemistry at Nottingham University, he studied Humanities at Leeds University.

He was ordained into the Western Buddhist order in Spain in 1992 and in 1993 moved to the north-east of England where he lectured in Chemistry and established Newcastle Buddhist Centre. His chapbook *Sublunary Voodoo* was published by MUDFOG in 1998, and since then he has worked primarily as a freelance writer, undertaking various commissions, residencies and creative writing teaching work.

He recently moved to Cumbria to establish a rural Buddhist centre and to continue exploring the relationship between art, Buddhism and western culture. He is currently writing an introduction to Buddhism.